RICHARD HUNDLEY
TEN SONGS
for High Voice and Piano

BOOSEY & HAWKES

AN IMAGEM COMPANY

DISTRIBUTED BY

Hal•Leonard®
CORPORATION
7777 W. BLUEMOUND RD. P.O. BOX 13819 MILWAUKEE, WI 53213

www.boosey.com
www.halleonard.com

COMPOSER'S NOTES

The melody for *Will There Really Be A Morning?* came to me as I read the poem for the first time. I tried to capture the wonderment and joy expressed in Dickinson's lovely poem.

In the mid-1960s I fell in love with the poems of John Fletcher (1579 – 1625) and set six of them to music. *Sweet River* was the first of these songs, and I think of it as a charming bubble— an invitation by the speaker (a river deity) to the beloved to "come live with me" with the promise that "not a wave shall trouble thee!"

When Children Are Playing Alone On The Green is a nostalgic song. My inspiration came from my childhood when I often played alone in the backyard of my grandmother's country house, and, as children do, invented an imaginary playmate.

Waterbird was originally composed as a choral movement in my cantata, *The Sea Is Swimming Tonight*, to poems by James Purdy. Upon hearing the cantata, tenor Paul Sperry requested an arrangement of *Waterbird* for solo voice, and I composed this romantic setting. Paul and pianist Irma Vallecillo gave the premiere.

Awake The Sleeping Sun was commissioned by Ethel Armeling, a singer and voice teacher in Michigan. Wishing to mark her 40th anniversary as a teacher by "something more than a party and a vacation trip," she asked me to write a song for her. The poem exalts the spirit, celebrating light over darkness.

When Virgil Thomson and I met we immediately took each other up with enthusiasm. For twenty-seven years, until his death, he was my friend and mentor. We shared similar backgrounds: he was from Missouri, and I, though born in Cincinnati, was reared in Kentucky. *A Package of Cookies* is a setting of a letter Virgil wrote to thank me for the gift of a tin of cookies. I could hear him speaking in the letter, and I was inspired to write his musical portrait. The song contains musical materials favored by the composer, including rows of triads built on the whole-tone scale, polytonality, and a paraphrase of an old hymn tune that children often sang in Bible class on Sunday, "Yes! Jesus Loves Me!"

Epitaph Of A Young Girl, like the two epitaph settings in my collection *Eight Songs* is mystical. The text is based on an inscription on a tombstone I came upon in the Boston Common.

After James Purdy wrote his poem ***Lions have lain in grasses before***, he immediately sent it to me. Scrawled at the top of the page was the admonition "Get yourself out of the moth balls and set this to music." However, I did not compose the music until several years later when I met the wonderful Lamar Alford, a flamboyant singing actor and scintillating Off-Broadway personality, for whom I wrote the song. Henri Rousseau's painting "Jungle With A Lion" in the Museum of Modern Art was my creative nourishment.

O My Darling Troubles Heaven With Her Loveliness is a passionate love song. Its expressive content requires some rubato and a wide range of dynamics and colors. This song is one of five songs commissioned by Joy In Singing for a concert of my music. Tenor Michael Ryan-Wenger and pianist Lydia Brown premiered the song.

Screw Spring is the humorous complaint of a girl who is not getting the attention she expects from her paramour. When I first met the poet and playwright William M. Hoffman, his work was being performed in the cafes and little theaters of Off-Off Broadway. His work was fresh, engaging, and contemporary, and I was especially attracted to his poetry. The song was first performed in concert by soprano Kate Hurney.

CONTENTS

This is a collection of individual songs for high voice which may be sung in any order or in combination with other songs the singer chooses. Most of the songs may be sung by both men and women and may be transposed to other keys.

Cover Design: Don Giordano, NYC
Portrait of the composer by Adam Berger, Boston

Will There Really Be A Morning?

Will there really be a morning?
Is there such a thing as day?
Could I see it from the mountains
If I were as tall as they?

Has it feet like water-lilies?
Has it feathers like a bird?
Is it brought from famous countries
of which I have never heard?

Oh, some scholar! Oh, some sailor!
Oh! some wise man from the skies!
Please to tell a little pilgrim
Where that place called morning lies!

Emily Dickinson

Sweet River

Do not fear to put thy feet
Naked in the river sweet;
Think not leech, or newt, or toad,
Will bite thy foot, when thou has trod;
Nor let the water rising high,
As thou wadest in, make thee cry
And sob; but ever live with me,
And not a wave shall trouble thee!

John Fletcher (1579-1625)

When Children Are Playing Alone
On The Green

When children are playing alone on the green,
In comes the playmate that never was seen.
When children are happy and lonely and good,
The Friend of the Children comes out of the wood.

Nobody heard him and nobody saw,
His is a picture you never could draw,
But he's sure to be present, abroad or at home,
When children are happy and playing alone.

Robert Louis Stevenson

Waterbird

Water bird, water bird
gently afloat,
know you my yearning
for places remote?

Water bird, water bird
under the sea,
keep you a kingdom
for sleepers like me?

James Purdy

Awake The Sleeping Sun

Come ye shepherds who have seen
Day's King deposed by Night's Queen.
Come lift we up our lofty song,
To wake the Sun that sleeps too long.

Welcome to our wondering sight
Eternity shut in a span!
Summer in Winter and Day in Night.
Heaven in Earth and God in man!

Verses from "The Nativity"
Richard Crashaw (1613-1649)

A Package Of Cookies

Dear Richard

A package of cookies lovely Danish cookies and
a thank-you note from me
a warmly enthusiastic thank-you note.
I wrote yesterday or rather mailed again a letter
I made a mistake about. I think I am about to
do
2 funny poems by Marianne Moore.
On principle, dinner Tuesday

Affectionately
Virgil T

Letter from Virgil Thomson

Epitaph Of A Young Girl

Short was my work
I sweetly rest
God took me home
when He saw best

I am not lost
I shall arise
when Christ, my Lord
descends the lower skies

Based on an inscription
on a tombstone in the Boston Common

Lions

Lions have lain in grasses before
& pale hares in lonely lanes,
but the trees and the leaves
& the leaves and the trees
are choicer and much more fair.

Abandon then lions
ignore pale hares
for with the trees and the leaves
  & the leaves and the trees
you've found your choicest fair
  by far choicest and fair.

James Purdy

O My Darling Troubles Heaven
With Her Loveliness

O my darling troubles heaven
With her loveliness

She is made of such cloth
That the angels cry to see her

Little gods dwell where she moves
And their hands open golden boxes
For me to lie in

She is built of lilies and candy doves
And the youngest star wakens in her hair

She calls me with the music of silver bells
And at night we step into other worlds

Like birds flying through the red and yellow air
Of childhood

O she touches me with the tips of wonder
And the angels cuddle like sleepy kittens
At our side

Kenneth Patchen

Screw Spring

Screw spring.
I'm the only thing not blooming.
The arrowhead plant,
so carelessly potted,
is growing godammit.
Even the jonquils,
bought for one dinner,
are not quite dead.
Under the bed
the dust is as thick
as wool on spring sheep,
which are undoubtedly
grazing where
grass is growing
at an enviable rate.

Screw spring.
My boyfriend's taken
to getting up early.
He goes out
to see plants
pushing their way
out of the ground,
and flowering,
and sits by some chartreuse tree
in the sun, breathing air
as sweet as berry wine,

watching girls pass.
Their faces are rested
from sleeping alone all winter.

Screw spring.
I wish it were winter,
when the world's
this one room.
These walls, this bed
do
not
grow.

William M. Hoffman

for Robert Wharton

Will There Really Be A Morning?

Emily Dickinson

Richard Hundley

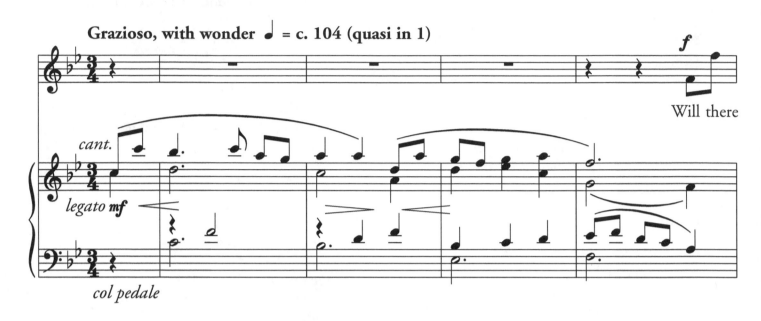

M-051-93348-8   Printed in U.S.A.

Oh, some wise man from the skies! ___ Please to tell a lit-tle

pil-grim Where that place ___ called Morn ___ ing,

OSSIA

Morn ___ ing lies! ___

where that place called Morn ___ ing lies! ___

OSSIA suitable for high, light sopranos *only*.

to Jeanette Scovotti
Sweet River

John Fletcher (1579-1625)

Richard Hundley

M-051-93348-8

Printed in U.S.A.

to Beverly Hoch

When Children Are Playing Alone On The Green

Robert Louis Stevenson

Richard Hundley

Andante, with a certain tenderness and mystery 𝅗𝅥. = c.40 (♩ = 120)

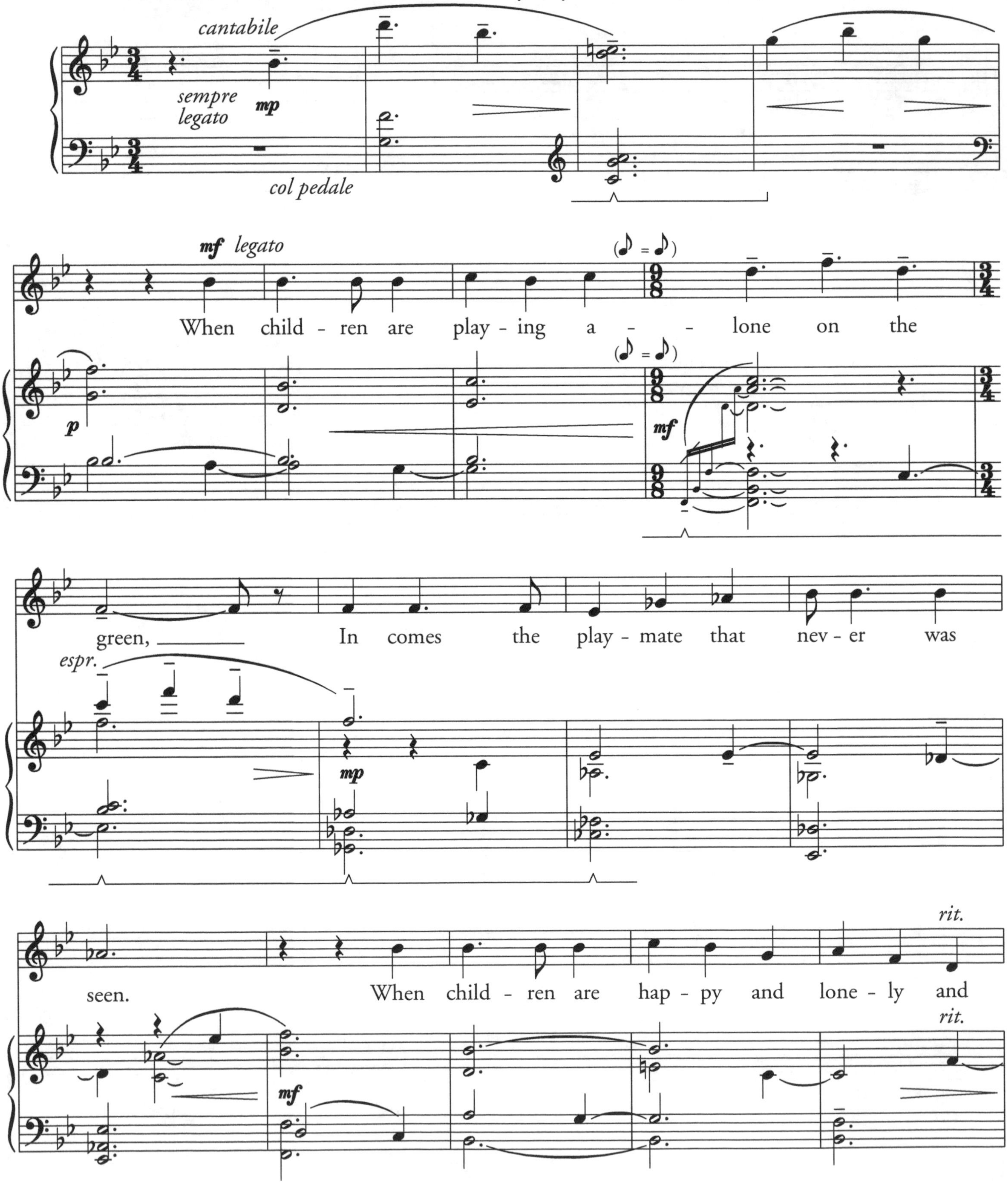

M-051-93348-8

Printed in U.S.A.

good, _____ The friend of the child – ren comes out of the

wood.

cantabile espressivo

No – bo – dy heard him and no – bo – dy saw, His is a

pic – ture you nev – er could draw. _____ But he's sure to be

to Paul Sperry

Waterbird

James Purdy

Richard Hundley

Wa- ter bird, wa - ter bird un - der the sea,_____ keep you a king - dom for sleep - ers like me, keep you a king - dom for sleep - ers _____ like ___ me?

a little more motion ♩ = 63

to Ethel Armeling

Awake The Sleeping Sun

Richard Crashaw (1613 - 1649)

Richard Hundley

M-051-93348-8

Printed in U.S.A.

Win - ter and Day in Night, Hea - ven in

Earth and God in man!

(bell)

Come ye shep-herds who have seen Day's King de - posed by Night's

Queen. Come lift we up our lof - ty song, To

wake___ the Sun that sleeps too long___ To

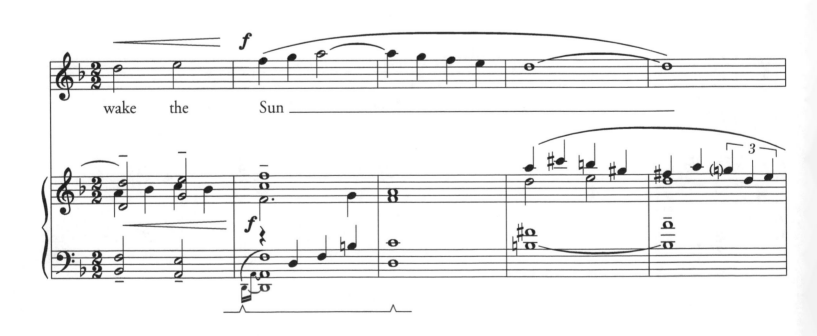

wake the Sun ___

that sleeps, _____ that sleeps _____ too

long, _____ that sleeps _____

return to **Tempo primo**

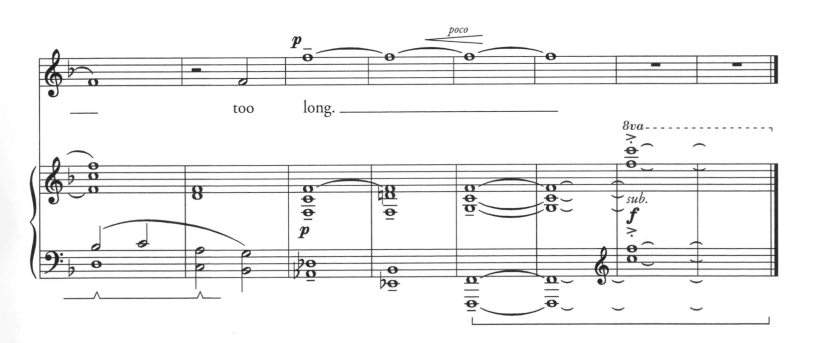

too long. _____

A Package Of Cookies

Virgil Thomson
(a letter to R.H., July 16, 1963)

Richard Hundley

The text is a letter by Virgil Thomson to Richard Hundley.
Used by permission of the Virgil Thomson Foundation.

M-051-93348-8   Printed in U.S.A.

thu - si - as - tic thank you note. I wrote yes-ter-day—

or rath-er mailed a-gain a let-ter I made a mis-take a-bout.

I think I am— a-bout to do

fun-ny poems by Ma-ri-anne Moore._____

senza pedale

joyfully,
marcata la melodia

On prin-ci-ple,

din - ner___ Tues - day._____

25

Epitaph Of A Young Girl

Based on an inscription on a
tombstone in the Boston Common

Richard Hundley

M-051-93348-8   Printed in U.S.A.

to Lamar Alford

Lions

James Purdy

Richard Hundley

Commissioned by *Joy In Singing*

O My Darling Troubles Heaven With Her Loveliness

Kenneth Patchen

Richard Hundley

And the an - gels cud-dle ___

like sleep-y ___ kit-tens ___ at our side. ___

Dec. 1998

to Kate Hurney and Iris Hiskey
Screw Spring

William M. Hoffman

Richard Hundley

Lively and rhythmic ♩ = 96 - 100

Screw spring.__ I'm __ the on-ly thing__ not bloom __ ing. The ar-row-head plant, so care-less-ly pot-ted, is grow __ ing god-dam-mit. E-ven the jon-quils, bought for one din-ner, are not quite dead.__

Un-der the bed the dust is as thick as wool on spring

mp

p legato *mp*

sheep, which are un-doubt-ed-ly graz — ing____ where grass is

mf

grow — — ing_____ at an en-vi-a-ble rate.

f

f

Screw spring. My boy-friend's ta-ken to get-ting up

mf

8va

mf *l.v.* *mp*

l.v.

molto espr.

quickly return to

world's __ this __ one _____ room. _____

mf legato

f

mf

mp

quickly return to

senza

Tempo primo

These walls, this bed do not __

f

grow. __

sub.
p

cresc.

mf

f

8va - - - - - - - - - - - -

cresc.

9

8va

f

ff

9

8ba

April 1968